I ♥ DAD!

An Odd Squad book for the world's best DAD!

RAVETTE PUBLISHING

First Published by
Ravette Publishing Limited 2006
PO Box 876, Horsham
West Sussex, RH12 9GH

Reprinted 2008, 2009, 2010, 2012, 2016

ISBN: 978-1-84161-395-6

Dug walked in to find his Dad trying to play his old records on the iPod.

Mum discovered the perfect way to get
Dad to go round the shops with her.

Billy made a mental note not to ask Dad
to help with his homework again.

Dad liked to do his best to make his daughter's new boyfriends feel comfortable.

When Dad wanted to treat Mum he bought
her a big bottle of bubbly.

The kids bought Dad the perfect jumper for his birthday.

Dad makes a cat flap.

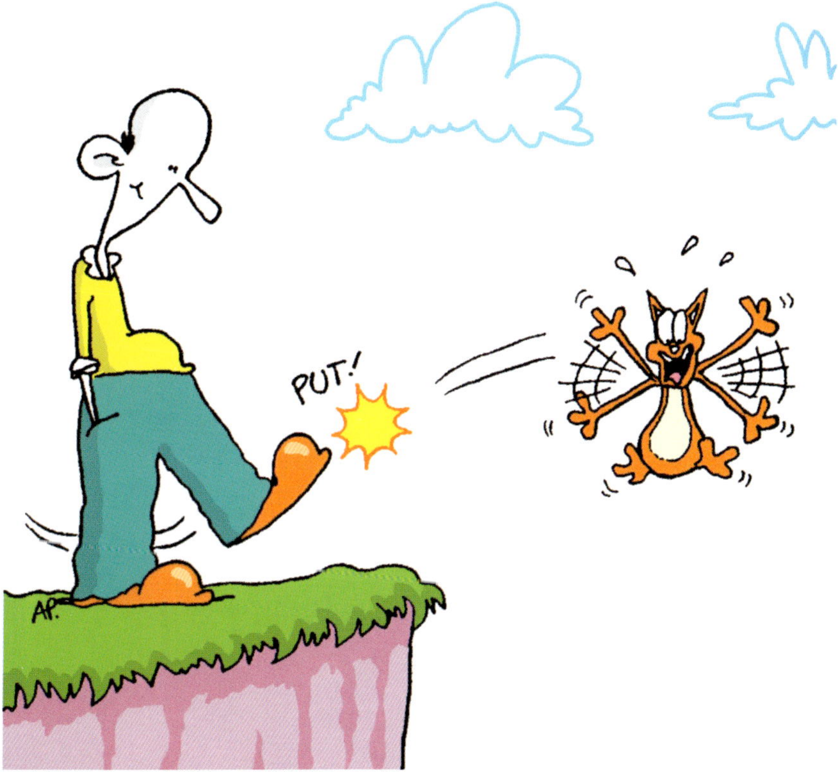
PUT!
AP.

Like all men, Dad handled having a cold really well.

Dad finally gets his perfect garden.

Dad had the perfect bedtime story to keep the kids quiet.

Dad was delighted that he'd taught their child his first word.

Dad would do anything to avoid doing the dishes.

Embarrassed by his balding, Dad gets some hair plugs.

The morning
after a heavy
session,
Dad woke up
with a terrible
hangover.

Sadly, Dad was unable to mow
the lawn that day.

As drunken Dad aimed the key for the 2549th time, he slowly began to weep.

Mum tried to persuade Dad that he was spending too much time on his mobile.

Dad discovered Mum had replaced the old dishwasher with a new model.

Once again, Dad was delighted to see the monthly phone bill arrive.

Fortunately, Dad had no need for expensive in-car satellite navigation.

Having followed the secret tunnel from a hole in Dad's shed, Mum wasn't altogether suprised where it came up.

Dad commented on how it seemed like only yesterday their little son couldn't talk or walk for himself.

Dad receives another perfect birthday gift from the kids.

Dad learns the perils of plucking nose hairs.

As a treat, Mum takes Dad to his favourite extra-hot curry house.

TOP TIPS FOR A DIY DAD

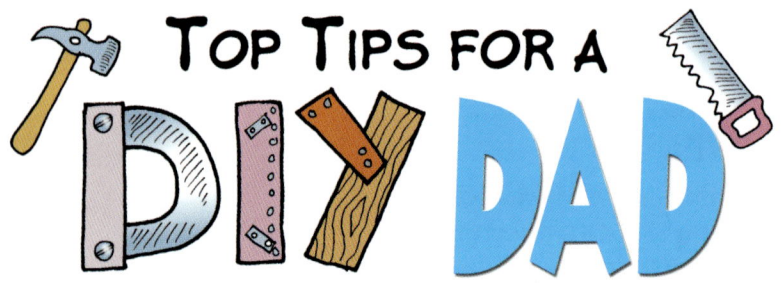

1.
BEFORE YOU BEGIN MAKE SURE YOU HAVE EVERYTHING YOU NEED.

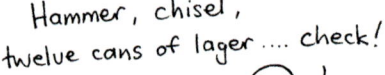

Hammer, chisel, twelve cans of lager .... check!

Mum, what's a "CLUCKING BELL"?

Er, nothing!

F****@©*..!!!

2.
ENTERTAIN THE FAMILY BY HITTING YOUR THUMB OCCASIONALLY AND SWEARING.

3.
ACT BUTCH BY COVERING YOUR FACE IN DIRT, MAKING MANLY GRUNTS AND LETTING OFF RASPERS!

4.
MASK ANY DODGY BITS OF D.I.Y. WITH A SELECTION OF PLANTS AND ORNAMENTS!

Billy learns not to leave Jimmy the tortoise lying around during one of Dad's D.I.Y. projects.

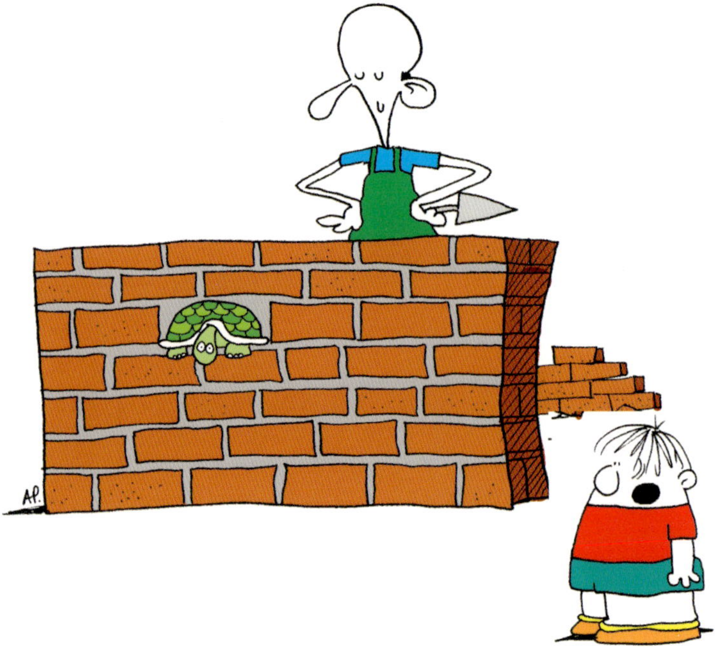
AP.

USES FOR
MY OLD MAN!

1.
BIG FAT BUMS MAKE EXCELLENT TRAMPOLINES FOR KIDDIES!

2.
STICK SEQUINS ON BALD HEADS TO MAKE A CHEAP DISCO BALL!

3.
SAGGY BITS ARE GREAT FOR STORING TINS AND BRIC-A-BRAC!

4.
EXCESS BUM HAIR CAN BE PULLED TAUT TO MAKE VIOLIN STRINGS!

Dad was most annoyed when he returned to his car, to find a big bird dropping on it.

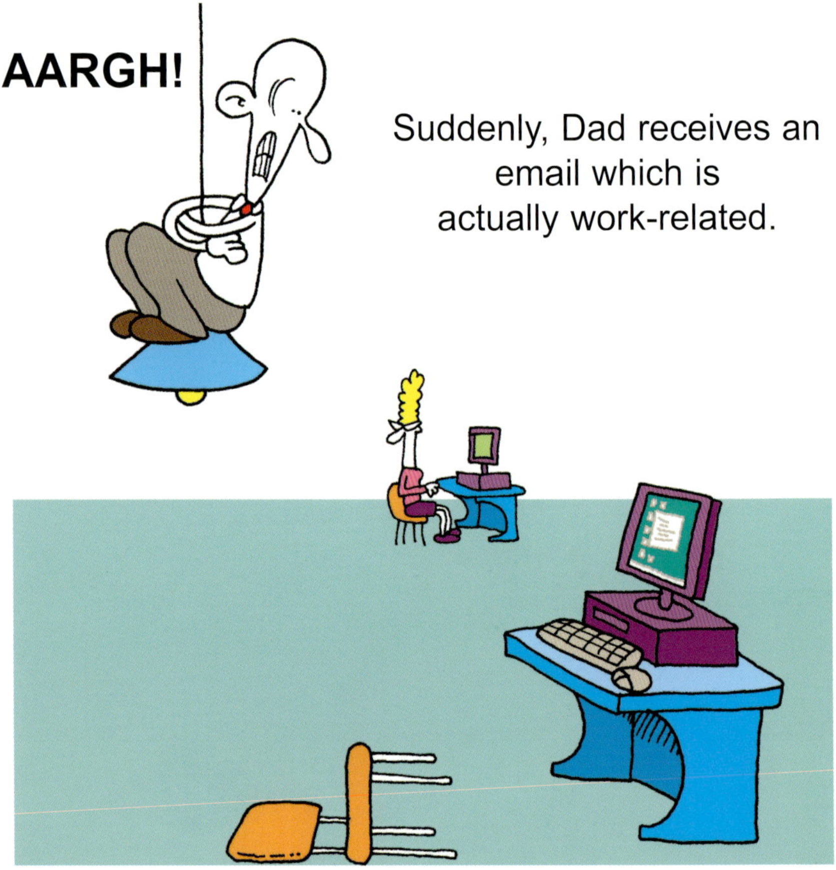
AARGH!

Suddenly, Dad receives an email which is actually work-related.

Dad's plan to sneak secretly into work late was ALMOST perfect.

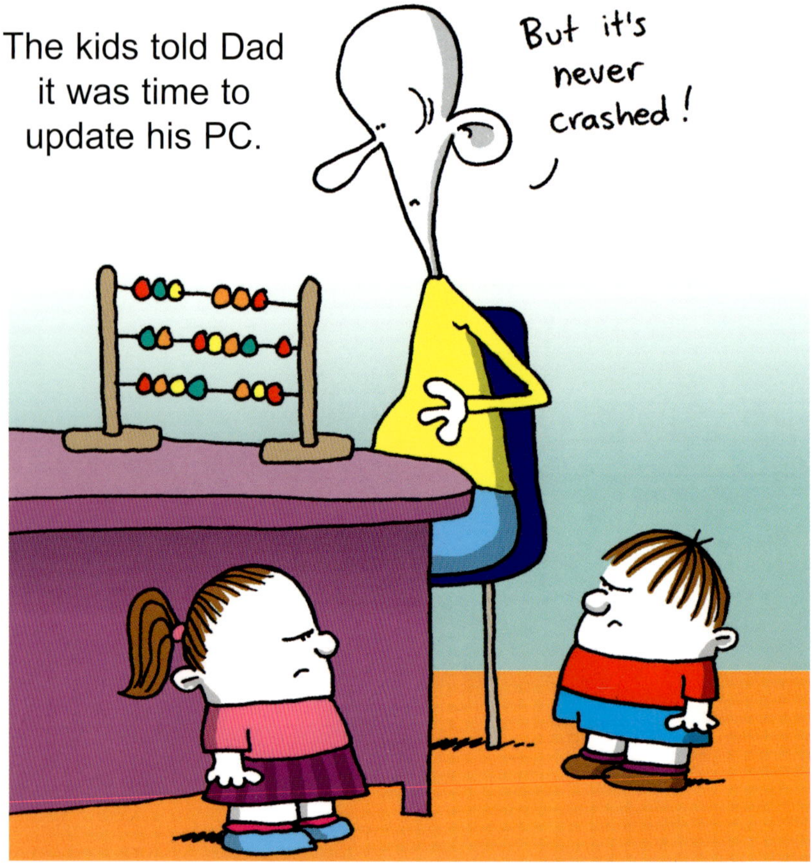
The kids told Dad it was time to update his PC.
But it's never crashed!

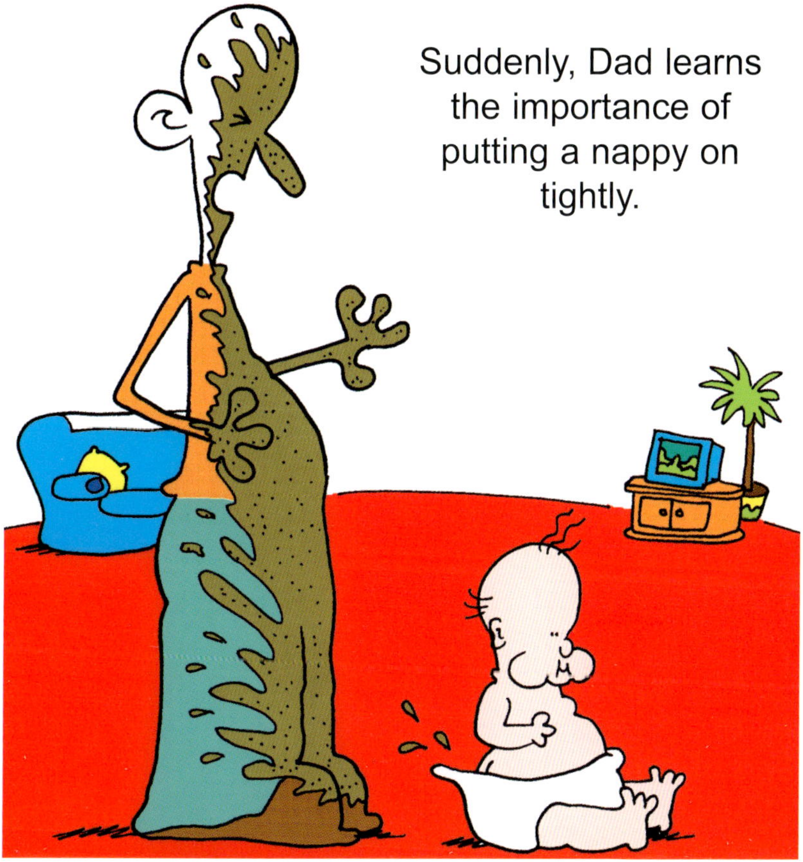
Suddenly, Dad learns the importance of putting a nappy on tightly.

Thanks to Dad's keen observation,
the boat swerved out of harm's way.

Dad always made sure he ate his five portions of veg each day.

Other ODD SQUAD hardback gift books available ...

		ISBN	Pri
Jeff's Dog - Diary of a bad dog	**(new)**	978-1-84161-386-4	£5.9
The Odd Squad's Kama Sutra	**(new)**	978-1-84161-385-7	£5.9
Cartoons to Cheer up a Grumpy Old Git		978-1-84161-360-4	£4.9
Cartoons to Cheer up a Stroppy Mare		978-1-84161-361-1	£4.9
I Love Beer		978-1-84161-238-6	£5.9
I Love Mum		978-1-84161-249-2	£5.9
I Love Poo		978-1-84161-394-9	£5.9
I Love Sex		978-1-84161-241-6	£4.9
I Love Wine		978-1-84161-239-3	£4.9
I Love Xmas		978-1-84161-262-1	£4.9

HOW TO ORDER:

Please send a cheque/postal order in £ sterling, made payable to 'Ravette Publishing'
for the cover price of the book/s and allow the following for post & packing ...

UK & BFPO	70p for the first book & 40p per book thereafter
Europe & Eire	£1.30 for the first book & 70p per book thereafter
Rest of the world	£2.20 for the first book & £1.10 per book thereafter

RAVETTE PUBLISHING LTD
PO Box 876, Horsham, West Sussex   RH12 9GH
Tel: 01403 711443   Fax: 01403 711554   Email: info@ravettepub.co.uk
www.ravettepublishing.tel

Prices and availability are subject to change without prior notice